EXTREME SCIENTISTS™
EXPLORING SPACE: ASTRONAUTS & ASTRONOMERS

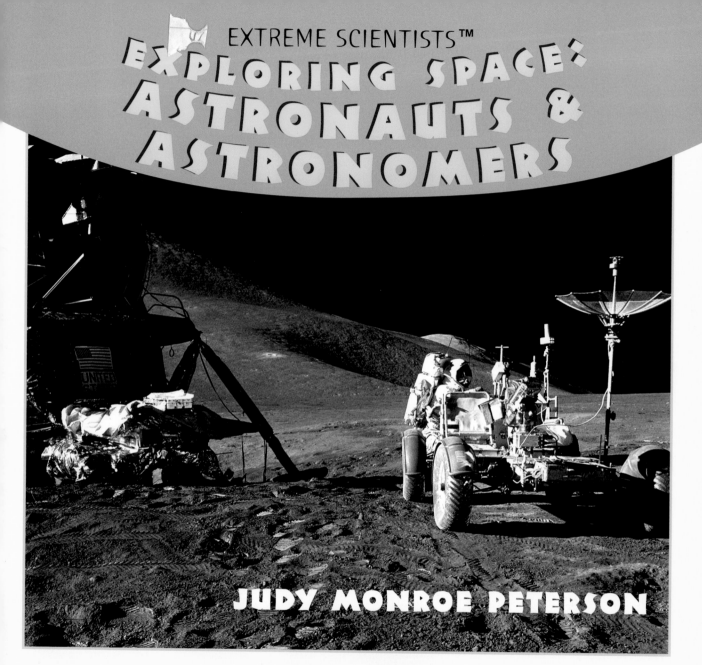

JUDY MONROE PETERSON

PowerKiDS press™

New York

To Dave—Keep Exploring!

Published in 2009 by The Rosen Publishing Group, Inc.
29 East 21st Street, New York, NY 10010

First Edition

Editor: Amelie von Zumbusch
Book Design: Kate Laczynski
Photo Researcher: Jessica Gerweck

Photo Credits: Cover, p. 1 © Johnson Space Center; pp. 5, 19, 21 © Getty Images; p. 7 © Peter Ginter/Getty Images; p. 9 © Lester Lefkowitz/Getty Images; pp. 11, 17 © NASA/Getty Images; p. 13 © NASA/JPL/University of Arizona; p. 15 © photojournal.

Library of Congress Cataloging-in-Publication Data

Peterson, Judy Monroe.
  Exploring space : astronauts & astronomers / Judy Monroe Peterson.
      p. cm. — (Extreme scientists)
  Includes index.
  ISBN 978-1-4042-4528-0 (library binding)
  1. Astronomy—Vocational guidance—Juvenile literature. 2. Astronautics—Vocational guidance—Juvenile literature. 3. Astronomers—Juvenile literature. 4. Astronauts—Juvenile literature. 5. Outer space—Exploration—Juvenile literature. I. Title.
  QB51.5.P48 2009
  500.5023—dc22
                                        2008010546

Manufactured in the United States of America

CONTENTS

Space Explorers

Do you like to look for stars and **planets** in the night sky? Perhaps you want to become an astronomer. Astronomers are scientists who study stars, moons, and planets. They study what these objects are made of, how they formed, and how they move through space. Sometimes, astronomers even discover new stars or planets!

If you dream about traveling through space and visiting the Moon or Mars, maybe being an astronaut is in your **future**. Astronauts are scientists who travel and **explore** space. Astronauts do many jobs, such as flying spacecraft or carrying out **experiments** in space. Astronauts have even walked on the Moon.

This astronomer is studying a map of the stars in the night sky. He is taking part in an effort to map a quarter of the sky, called the Sloan Digital Sky Survey.

The Wonders of Space

Some astronomers spend their time studying stars. These scientists have learned that our **galaxy**, the Milky Way, has **billions** of stars. Stars come in different sizes and colors. Some stars are small and red, while other stars are giant and blue. Our Sun is a medium-sized, yellow star.

Other astronomers study the planets in our **solar system**. They send spacecraft to explore the planets and their moons. These spacecraft study the weather, rocks, and soil there. They try to find out if plants or animals ever lived on these planets and moons.

DID YOU KNOW?

Astronomers also learn about space by studying meteorites, or rocks from space that have crashed into Earth. Meteorites give scientists clues to how the solar system formed.

The astronomer Vera Rubin made important discoveries about how galaxies move. Here, she points to a picture of the Andromeda Galaxy.

Cool Tools Astronomers Use

Many astronomers work in labs called observatories. There, scientists use books, charts, computers, and large **telescopes** to study space. Several kinds of telescopes pick up waves. Every space object gives off different kinds of waves. Optical telescopes see light waves. Radio telescopes sense radio waves. Information, or facts, from the telescopes goes into large computers for astronomers to study.

Astronomers have learned a lot about space from light waves and radio waves. Starlight can show astronomers what a star is made of and where and how fast the star is moving. Astronomers have used radio telescopes to make maps of hot and cold spots on Mercury and other planets.

This astronomer is setting up a large telescope. Telescopes need to be carefully directed toward the part of the sky that scientists plan to study.

9

The Giant Hubble Telescope

A blanket of gases called an atmosphere covers Earth. This atmosphere makes objects in space look fuzzy when people look at them through telescopes from Earth. To see space objects clearly, scientists built the Hubble Space Telescope. This huge telescope **orbits** Earth beyond our planet's atmosphere.

The Hubble Space Telescope travels around Earth every 96 minutes, taking clear pictures of space objects. Astronomers on Earth can direct the telescope where to look. The telescope sends these pictures to astronomers on Earth. Scientists store the pictures in large computers to study later.

DID YOU KNOW?

The Hubble Space Telescope has supplied astronomers with many wonderful pictures. Some pictures show galaxies moving. Sometimes these galaxies are crashing into each other. Other pictures show new stars forming.

The Hubble Space Telescope, seen here, orbits about 380 miles (610 km) above Earth. The big telescope began orbiting Earth in 1990.

A Red Planet Called Mars

Most planets are too far away to visit in person. Therefore, astronomers often use telescopes to study planets. Astronomers also send spacecraft to planets to learn more about them. In 2004, the *Opportunity* and *Spirit* spacecraft landed on Mars, the fourth planet from the Sun.

Opportunity and *Spirit* have studied Mars's rocks and soil. The spacecraft send information to scientists on Earth. Scientists have discovered dead, giant **volcanoes** on Mars. Astronomers have also learned that salty water once flowed on the **surface** of Mars. Today, dust and iron cover Mars. The iron on Mars makes the planet look red when seen through telescopes.

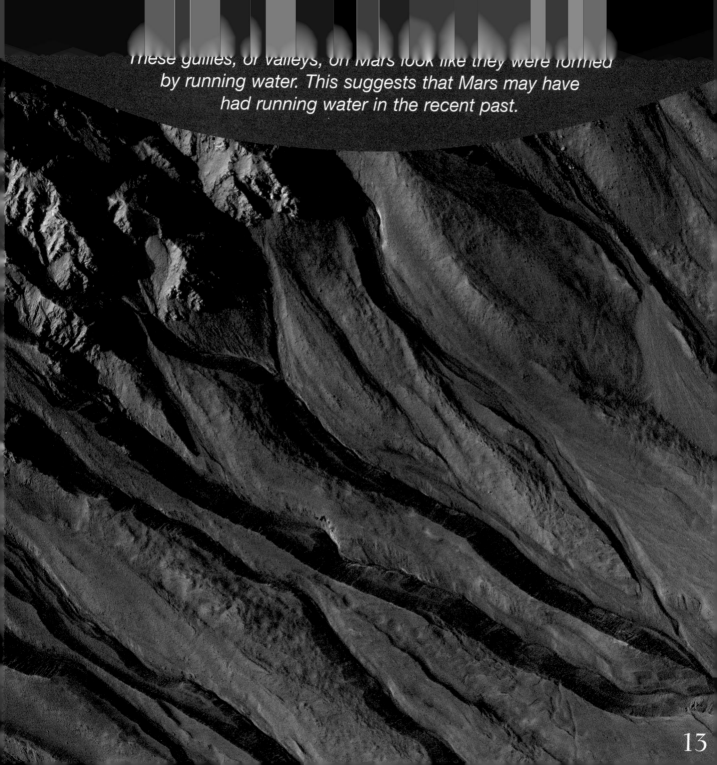

These gullies, or valleys, on Mars look like they were formed by running water. This suggests that Mars may have had running water in the recent past.

To learn more about Saturn, the sixth planet from the Sun, astronomers blasted the *Cassini-Huygens* spacecraft into space in 1977. In 2004, *Cassini-Huygens* reached Saturn, and the two parts of the spacecraft, *Cassini* and *Huygens*, separated. *Cassini* began orbiting Saturn and sending back pictures to Earth. These pictures taught scientists that Saturn is made mostly of gas and has seven main rings. These flat, wide rings are made of ice, dust, and rock.

After separating from *Cassini*, *Huygens* headed toward Titan, the largest of Saturn's more than 30 moons. *Huygens* landed on Titan in 2005. It learned that Titan has an orange surface and is covered by orange clouds.

Saturn, seen here, has the largest and best-known ring system in our solar system. However, several other planets, such as Jupiter and Uranus, also have rings.

Working in Space

While planets are too far away for astronomers to study in person, some scientists do go into space. Astronauts do many different jobs on a spaceflight. Some astronauts fly spacecraft. Others keep spacecraft running smoothly or work on tools, such as space telescopes. Astronauts have even fixed the Hubble Space Telescope.

Astronauts also fix broken satellites in space. Satellites are tools that orbit Earth and gather information. Scientists use some satellites to study space. Satellites also help people, ships, and planes from getting lost and send telephone calls across oceans.

DID YOU KNOW?

Astronauts are carefully trained to live in space. They ride in special airplanes and practice doing space jobs under water. Moving underwater is a bit like floating in space.

This astronaut is working on the International Space Station, or ISS, a craft that orbits Earth. People stay on the ISS for several months at a time and carry out experiments there.

Living in Space Shuttles

Astronauts travel and live in spacecraft called shuttles. Shuttles look like large airplanes. Like people on Earth, astronauts in shuttles must breathe, sleep, eat, exercise, and use the bathroom. However, everything is done differently in space.

On Earth, a force called gravity keeps things on the ground. Space has very low gravity, so objects in space weigh almost nothing. Therefore, people, food, water, and tools float in space. In a shuttle, beds are tied down. Astronauts clean their bodies with wet wipes. They drink through tubes to keep drops from floating around.

DID YOU KNOW?

Space is very cold and has no air for people to breathe. When they go outside their shuttles, astronauts wear space suits that give them air to breathe and keep them warm.

These astronauts are eating their breakfast. The yellow object floating in front of the astronaut on the left is a piece of cheese!

Space Experiments

On some spaceflights, astronauts do science experiments in space shuttles. There are many experiments that can be done only in the low gravity of space. For example, astronauts study ways to make very strong metals and try out new **medicines**.

In other experiments, astronauts see what happens to people, animals, and plants in space. Some astronauts spend months in space and carefully record what happens to their bodies. Astronauts have found that their bones and **muscles** waste away in low gravity because they have little to do. Scientists try to discover the foods and exercises they need to stay strong in space.

This astronaut is working in a research module, or part of the spacecraft specially set up to do experiments in space.

Becoming an Astronomer or Astronaut

If you are interested in space, study the stars and planets in the night sky. You can read books or visit **planetariums** to learn more. Try looking at some of the great space exploration Web sites on the Internet, too. Some kids even go to space camp, where they wear space suits, eat space food, and visit a shuttle.

To become an astronomer or astronaut, you have to learn lots of math, science, and computer science. Though these jobs take lots of work, they offer the chance to make great discoveries. If you decide to become an astronaut or astronomer, you might someday walk on Mars or discover a new kind of star!

GLOSSARY

billions (BIL–yunz) Thousands of millions. One billion is 1,000 millions.

experiments (ik–SPER–uh–ments) Sets of actions or steps taken to learn more about something.

explore (ek–SPLOR) To go over carefully.

future (FYOO–chur) The time that is coming.

galaxy (GA–lik–see) A large group of stars and the planets that circle them.

medicines (MEH–duh–sinz) Drugs that doctors give to help fight illness.

muscles (MUH–sulz) Parts of the body that make the body move.

orbits (OR–bits) Travels in a circular path.

planetariums (pla–neh–TER–ee–umz) Places for looking at images of the night sky.

planets (PLA–nets) Large objects, such as Earth, that move around stars.

solar system (SOH–ler SIS–tem) A group of planets that circles a star.

surface (SER–fes) The outside of anything.

telescopes (TEH–leh–skohps) Tools used to make faraway objects appear closer and larger.

volcanoes (vol–KAY–nohz) Openings in a planet that sometimes shoot up hot, melted rock, called lava.

WEB SITES

Due to the changing nature of Internet links, PowerKids Press has developed an online list of Web sites related to the subject of this book. This site is updated regularly. Please use this link to access the list:
www.powerkidslinks.com/exsci/astron/